Capstone Short Biographies

African-American Scientists

Robert Jones, Reatha Clark King,
Walter Massey, Franklyn G. Prendergast,
Larry Shannon

by Jetty St. John

CAPSTONE PRESS

MANKATO

C A P S T O N E   P R E S S
818 North Willow Street • Mankato, MN 56001

Printed in the United States of America.

Library of Congress Cataloging-in Publication Data
St. John, Jetty.
    African-American scientists/by Jetty St. John
    p. cm.
    Includes bibliographical references and index.
    Summary: Brief biographies of five African-American scientists of this
century.
    ISBN 1-56065-358-2
    1. Scientists--United States--Biography--Juvenile literature. 2. Afro-
American scientists--Biography--Juvenile literature. [1. Scientists. 2. Afro-
Americans--Biography.] I. Title.
Q141.K247 1996
509'.2'273--dc20

                                                                    95-47864
                                                                         CIP
                                                                          AC

Photo credits
University of Minnesota, Bruce Challgren: 6
Mayo Clinic: cover and 8
University of Minnesota: John Slivon, 11
Ciba-Geigy Corporation: 22
University of Minnesota, Tom Foley: 30

Table of Contents

Words in **boldface** type in the text are defined in the Glossary in the back of this book.

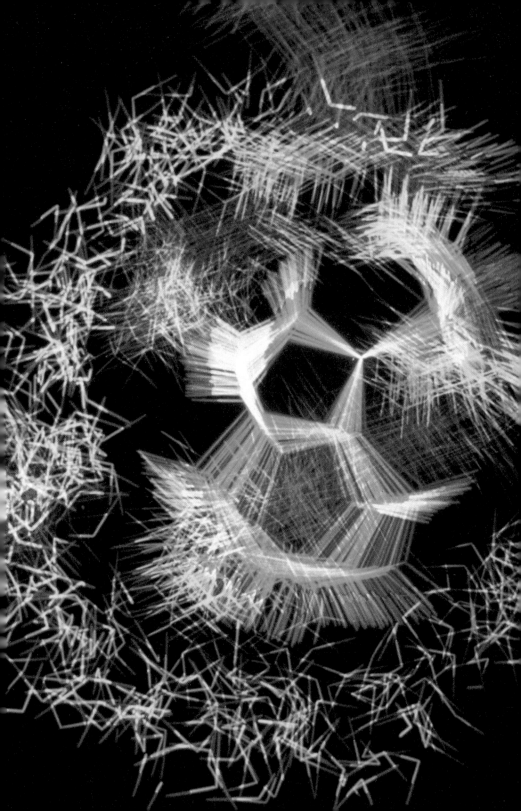

Chapter 1

What Is a Scientist?

Scientists are curious about the world. They ask many questions. They talk to other people with the same questions. All of them are looking for answers.

When scientists cannot find an answer, they make a guess. The guess is called a hypothesis. Scientists do experiments to test the hypothesis.

If an experiment works, the scientist tells other people about it. Often they write articles about the experiment for science magazines.

Scientists use computers to study protein molecules, which appear as colorful designs.

Other scientists repeat the original experiment. If everyone gets the same results, the hypothesis is accepted as a fact.

At Work

Scientists study birds, animals, and plants. They study the weather, stars, rocks, heat, and light. They study anything in the natural world. Scientists often work in teams.

Scientists learn even when experiments go wrong. They never give up searching for answers.

African-American Scientists

This book will introduce you to five African-American scientists. They are from many different places. They decided to become scientists for different reasons. They are experts in different fields. They all enjoy being scientists and helping others through their work.

Plant physiologist Robert Jones explains to middle school student Sean French how corn grows.

Chapter 2

Franklyn G. Prendergast

Franklyn Prendergast was born in Linstead, Jamaica, in 1945. He lived with his mother and four older brothers and sisters.

Two of his uncles were doctors. They had trained in the United States. This impressed Prendergast.

But Prendergast lived in the middle of a banana plantation. The world of medicine seemed far away.

Franklyn Prendergast uses laser beams and computers at Mayo Clinic to study bacteria and viruses.

Prendergast loved learning. Science classes made him curious about the natural world. He wondered why the farm animals got sick. He wondered why chickens had reddish feathers and why ducks laid green eggs.

When he was 18, Prendergast went to medical school at the University of the West Indies. He became a doctor. But he wanted to learn more. So he went to Oxford University in England.

Graduated With Honors

His classes taught him more than facts. He also learned how to think through problems. He graduated with an honor's degree in physiology, which is the study of animals and their parts.

Prendergast wanted to learn about **molecules.** These are some of the smallest known elements. He moved to the United States to get a **doctorate** in biochemistry, which is the study of the chemistry of plants and animals.

Franklyn Prendergast wants to understand how protein molecules work.

For his doctorate work, Prendergast went to the University of Minnesota. He also started working at the famous Mayo Clinic in Rochester, Minnesota.

Using Lasers

Today, Prendergast uses **laser beams** and computers at the Mayo Clinic. He studies how **bacteria** and **viruses** affect the human body. He tries to find new medicines to treat all kinds of diseases.

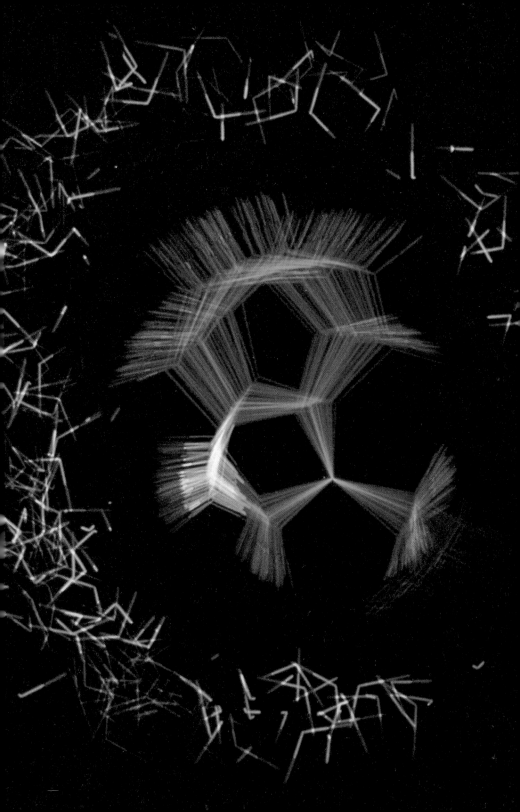

All parts of the body are made up of molecules. The tiny parts of a molecule move quickly. Prendergast uses a laser beam to track and measure the parts of a molecule.

He uses the measurements to make computer pictures. The pictures show the structure and movement of the molecules. That way he can study them better.

Fighting Bacteria and Viruses

Prendergast wants to understand how **protein** molecules work. Then he can learn how bacteria and viruses work because they are also made up of proteins.

His goal is to discover weak spots in the surfaces of bacteria and viruses. Then he can find drugs to target these areas. The drugs can attach to the bacteria or viruses. Then the bacteria or viruses cannot harm the body.

If scientists know how protein molecules work, then they can learn how bacteria and viruses work.

Chapter 3

Larry Shannon

Larry Shannon was born in Florida in 1933. He grew up with eight brothers and sisters. He often slipped away to visit his grandparents. They had a farm in Palmetto, Florida. He spent hours looking for crayfish, minnows, salamanders, and turtles in his grandparents' pond.

As he grew older, Shannon learned that fish were dying because of chemical pollution in many nearby rivers and lakes. Some of these chemicals were **pesticides** that drained off the farmland.

Larry Shannon observes fish in a tank to see if any abnormal behavior occurs.

Shannon went to college when he was 16. He wanted to learn more about plants and animals. He received a degree in biology from Florida A & M University. Biology is the study of living things.

Ocean Animals

Shannon visited the ocean and saw that wildlife was in danger. Birds got tangled in fishing lines and plastic six-pack holders. Oil got into their feathers. They could not fly.

Seals with oil in their fur could not keep warm, so they died. Some fish died because they had eaten plastic. The plastic came from bags floating in the water.

In a lab, Shannon discovered that many fish had high levels of **mercury** in them. He decided that people should know that rivers and oceans were polluted. They should know that some animals and plants could become **extinct.**

Larry Shannon analyzes the quality of water from a fish tank. He teaches at the University of Maryland.

Learning and Working

Shannon wanted to learn more. First he got a **master's degree** in biology and science education from Atlanta University. In 1971, he went to Iowa State University.

Shannon graduated in 1974 with a doctorate in aquatic toxicology. That is the study of poisons in bodies of water and their effect on plants and animals. Shannon worked at Iowa State and Livingstone College in Salisbury, North Carolina. Then he got a job in Washington, D.C., supervising water research projects.

He talked with researchers throughout the country. He asked them to share ideas about how to clean up the nation's waterways. He helped set government regulations that protected rivers and oceans from more pollution.

Dioxins

Shannon studies dioxins, which are poisonous waste products. Some industries dump dioxins into rivers.

In the water, dioxins are absorbed by plants and **plankton.** Small fish eat plankton. The dioxins build up in their bodies.

Larger fish eat the small fish. Then the large fish are eaten by birds, animals, and people. More poison builds up in creatures that are higher up on the **food chain.**

Safe Fish

Over time, poisonous chemicals can build up in humans. If pregnant women eat fish with poisons in them, their babies might have birth defects. Some people might get cancer.

Many government departments warn people about how much fish it is safe to eat. Too much fish could be dangerous. People in some areas can eat more fish than in others. Shannon lived in California for two years and studied which fish were safe to eat.

Fish and Game Management

In 1983, Shannon moved to Minnesota. He became the director of fisheries and wildlife at the state Department of Natural Resources. He helped set rules to limit fishing and hunting.

In Minnesota and other states, many young fish from hatcheries are released into rivers and lakes every year. Figuring out what types of fish to release is tricky. If new breeds are introduced, they can take over the food and habitat of the fish that are already there. Then the fish that were there first die. Shannon managed and restocked more than 6,000 fishing lakes.

Teaching

Shannon went back to Washington, D.C., after working in Minnesota. He worked for the Department of Fish and Wildlife for five years. First he was chief of endangered species and then chief of fisheries management.

Today, Shannon teaches at the University of Maryland, Eastern Shore. He encourages his students to preserve the environment. He wants children to be able to search for salamanders in ponds the way he did. He wants people to be able to eat the fish they catch. A safe environment helps plants, animals, and people stay healthy.

Larry Shannon examines fish tissue to see if there are any abnormal cells.

Chapter 4

Reatha Clark King

Reatha Clark King was born in 1938. She grew up in Pavo, Georgia. Like many other African-American children, she had to work in the cotton fields. They worked even if it meant they had to miss school.

Her mother, Ola Mae Clark, only went to school until the third grade. Her father, Willie Clark, never learned to read or write.

When King was seven years old, she was sent to live with her grandmother, Mamie Watts. Her mother moved north to find better-paying jobs. Her father became a migrant

Reatha Clark King was named an exceptional black scientist in 1984 by the Ciba-Geigy Corporation.

worker. He moved from place to place harvesting crops.

King learned to read and write at school and through her church. She wrote letters to her uncles who were fighting in World War II. She wrote to her mother.

School and Work

When King's mother returned, she still had trouble finding work. King and her two sisters were always moving to different schools. They followed their mother while she searched for better jobs.

When she was 12, King went to the Moultrie High School for Negro Youth in Moultrie, Georgia. She enjoyed learning. But because she came from a poor family, other students made fun of her. King tried not to let this bother her.

She had to help support her family. She worked after school as a maid. She painted broom handles in a factory. She also worked in the fields.

King received a scholarship to attend Clark College in Atlanta. She loved school. She

Reatha Clark King was elected as homecoming queen at Clark College in Atlanta in 1958.

studied all kinds of subjects, including art and drama.

Her family wanted her to become a home economics teacher. They wanted her to come home to teach. It took courage for her to tell them she would rather study chemistry.

King received a degree in biology from Clark. Her relatives were upset. They thought she was becoming too smart. They worried that no man would want to marry her.

The University of Chicago

King went to the University of Chicago to study chemistry when she was 20. She was excited. Getting an education was a way to escape being poor.

Her time at the University of Chicago was not always easy. She missed her family and friends. There were not many women in her classes. Chicago winters were bitterly cold. She wrote home, begging her mother to send long underwear.

For her doctorate, King studied the effect of heat on alloys. They are a mixture of two or more metals.

A year before King graduated, she married a math and science teacher named N. Judge King. They moved to Washington, D.C., where she got her first job at the National Bureau of Standards.

She studied materials to see if they would wear away if exposed to chemicals and intense

Reatha Clark King worked in the laboratory at the National Bureau of Standards in Washington, D.C.

heat. She was trying to find a way to handle chemicals safely.

King invented a special coiled tube. It allows extremely hot liquids to cool properly so they do not blow up. Her research helped people develop the materials that line a rocket's fuel system.

A Life of Helping People

After six years in Washington, King's husband got a doctorate in chemistry. The family moved to New York when he was offered a job there. By this time, the Kings had two small boys, Jay and Scott.

In New York, King started a new job. She taught school in the inner city. She thought that an education could help a lot of people.

Soon after they moved, her father died. King knew his life had been hard because he had not had an education. So she devoted her life to helping people in need.

In 1976, King received a master's degree in business administration from Columbia University in New York City. In 1977, she

Reatha Clark King participated in the inaugural ceremony of Thomas Stark as president of Winona State University in Minnesota.

became president of Metropolitan State University in Minneapolis, Minnesota. She helped increase the number of women going to school there.

Today, she is the president of the General Mills Foundation in Minnesota. There, she uses the skills she learned while growing up and those she learned as a scientist. She helps people get food, shelter, and schooling.

Chapter 5

Robert Jones

Robert Jones was born in 1951. He grew up in Dawson, Georgia. His parents were sharecroppers. They paid the rent with part of the crops they raised. Every day after school, Jones helped with the family work. He tended fields of peanuts and cotton.

Often Jones got into trouble for daydreaming. He would stare at a leaf and wonder why it had veins. When he ate peanuts, he tried to figure out how they got inside a shell.

Jones wanted a chemistry set. His family could not afford to buy him one. So he created his own experiments. He made a volcano by mixing baking soda with food dye and vinegar.

Robert Jones and a student intern at the University of Minnesota study an ear of corn. They are working to improve the corn's food value.

Sometimes Jones came up with crazy inventions. He made a scooter from junk he found on the farm. He used wheels, spark plugs, pieces of wire, and string.

Jones went to college near his home. He did not have very much money. He worked at several part-time jobs.

He worked for a rubber manufacturing company. He learned how to be a meat carver at a grocery store. He was a lab assistant.

Jones earned enough money to support his wife and baby. It was hard to study, have a family, and work so much. But he did it.

Helping Things Grow

At college, Jones saw how **fertilizer** could make corn grow better. He set up experiments in the lab. He gave young corn plants different amounts of fertilizer. He wanted to see what worked the best.

When he was 22, Jones knew what he wanted to do with his life. He wanted to grow crops and study plants. First he studied

I often got into trouble for day-dreaming. I sat wondering how peanuts got inside the shell. Other times I stood..

University of Minnesota artist Jeffrey Jones drew the many faces of science for a campus exhibit.

peanuts. He found that adding **calcium** helped them grow properly.

Then he began work to improve grass. He wanted to make better grazing land for cattle.

When he was 27, he earned a doctorate in crop science.

Jones found a job as a professor at the University of Minnesota. He worked with his students to grow corn with more starch in the kernels. This gives the corn more food value.

He researched ways that plants could survive better in hot climates. In Mexico and other warm parts of the world, he helped people grow better crops to feed their families and animals.

South Africa

Jones never forgot his childhood. He remembered growing up poor. He remembered living in the South, where blacks could not go to school with whites. They could not eat at the same restaurants or even ride the same buses.

These memories came back when he traveled to South Africa. Until recently, blacks in South Africa were forced by law to live apart from whites. They could not vote, own land, travel, or work without permits.

Robert Jones hopes to develop a supercorn to feed people around the world.

Robert Jones helped Mexican farmers grow corn that will survive in harsh conditions.

At first Jones did not want to go to South Africa. Then he decided it was a way to help thousands of blacks get an education. He wanted to help black students get into colleges in North America.

More Than a Scientist

Jones found his work rewarding, but he was lonely in Minnesota. He joined a singing group called the Sounds of Blackness. They sing all kinds of music, from African chants to rhythm and blues.

The group has won a Grammy award. Its members sang background music for the movie *Batman Returns.*

Jones has worked with other volunteers to organize food basket programs. The volunteers gather food that would otherwise be wasted. They use vans to pick up extra food from restaurants. These dinners are delivered to homeless shelters instead of going to waste.

Jones's dream is to develop a supercorn to feed people around the world. The supercorn would be able to survive tough growing conditions. Jones hopes that science will make his dream a reality.

Chapter 6

Walter Massey

Walter Massey was born in 1938. He and his younger brother lived with their parents in Hattiesburg, Mississippi. His mother taught grade school. She encouraged Massey to read all kinds of books.

Science fiction stories were his favorite. He especially liked stories about airplane pilots. Massey also played the saxophone and thought of being a musician. He loved number puzzles, too. He could not do enough of them.

Massey was accepted at Morehouse College in Atlanta after he finished the 10th grade. He was very good at math. Suddenly, he found himself among students from all over the world.

Walter Massey worked to produce temperatures close to absolute zero.

He did not think he was as smart as the other students. He could not express himself as clearly as he wanted. He called his mother and asked her to get him out of college.

Massey's mother persuaded him to talk to his physics professor. Massey liked him and listened to him. Soon he began to work through a high school English textbook. He practiced correct pronunciation when he was waiting for the bus or taking a shower.

Absolute Zero

At college, Massey learned what happens to things at very low temperatures. Water turns to ice. Gases change to liquids. An orange, after it is dipped in extremely cold **liquid nitrogen,** shatters like glass when dropped.

Massey earned a bachelor of science degree in physics and math. When he was 20, he made it his goal to work in the country's top research labs. He wanted to produce temperatures close to **absolute zero,** the temperature at which atoms stop moving.

Walter Massey, right, his wife, Shirley Massey, and the Rev. Otis Moss stand in front of a portrait of Martin Luther King Jr. Moss is chairman of the board of Morehouse College, where Massey is president.

Keeping his goal in mind, Massey spent six years in St. Louis, Missouri. He got his master's and doctorate degrees in physics at Washington University. He used **liquid helium** to reach extremely low temperatures. This slowed down the motion of atoms.

When atoms nearly stop moving, researchers can study them. They can see what the atoms look like. They can figure out how they are put together.

When scientists know how atoms are put together, they can create new materials. These new materials do not appear in nature. They can be used to make many things.

Some cars are made of an artificial material called carbon fiber. It springs back to its original shape after a ding. Some tennis rackets are made with graphite. It can hold its shape, but it is also flexible enough to take a hard serve.

Massey worked at the famous Argonne National Laboratory in Chicago. Later he became the director of Argonne. He was also the vice president for research at the University of Chicago.

Superconductivity

The Argonne lab studies ways to use energy efficiently. At extremely low temperatures, electricity can flow through a material with little or no **resistance**. This is called **superconductivity**.

Scientists would like to use superconductivity to get electricity into homes without losing any of it in the power lines. They are also building electric motors that can run for a long time.

With superconductivity it is possible for trains to fly just above special tracks. These trains are three times faster than regular trains. They can go 300 miles (480 kilometers) per hour. They are already used in Germany and Japan.

More Than a Scientist

Massey has been the director of the National Science Foundation in Washington, D.C. His work there has helped young people around the country get a better science education. The foundation also helps scientists get the money they need for research.

Massey has received more than 20 honorary doctorate degrees from colleges all over the country. He returned to Morehouse College where his physics professor believed in him and encouraged him to stay in school. He is now the president there.

Glossary

absolute zero—the coldest temperature possible for matter, which is minus 273.16 degrees Celsius or minus 459.69 degrees Fahrenheit. In theory, atoms stop moving at this temperature. Scientists have yet to make anything this cold.

bacteria—one-celled organisms that can cause diseases

calcium—essential part of bones, shells, and teeth

doctorate—the highest degree awarded by a college or university

extinct—when something no longer exists

fertilizer—material that improves the quality of the soil or increases plant growth

food chain—series of animals and plants in which each kind serves as food for the next in the series

laser beam—a narrow, intense beam of light used for surgery, cutting metal, communications, research, and measuring devices

liquid helium—the liquid state of helium, when it is below minus 268.9 degrees Celsius (minus 452.02 Fahrenheit), which is the lowest known point at which an element turns from a gas into a liquid

liquid nitrogen—the liquid state of nitrogen, a tasteless, odorless, colorless gas, when it is below minus 195.8 degrees Celsius (minus 320.4 Fahrenheit)

mercury—silver-colored metallic chemical element

master's degree—a college or university degree awarded after graduate study

molecules—the smallest part of an element that can exist and still keep the characteristics of the element

pesticide—chemical used to kill weeds and insects

plankton—tiny plant and animal life that drifts in the oceans and is used as food

protein—one class of molecules found in the cells of all living creatures

resistance—the force that opposes the flow of electricity

superconductivity—occurs at extremely low temperatures, when electricity flows through a material with little or no resistance

viruses—things that infect animals, plants, and bacteria, causing diseases

To Learn More

Cooper, Christopher. *Matter.* New York: Dorling Kindersley, 1992.

Elting, Mary. *The Macmillan Book of the Human Body.* New York: Aladdin Books, 1986.

Kramer, Stephen. *How to Think Like a Scientist.* New York: Thomas Y. Crowell, 1987.

Schwartz, David M. *The Hidden Life of the Pond.* New York: Crown, 1988.

Waters, Marjorie. *The Victory Garden Kid's Book.* Boston: Houghton Mifflin Co., 1988.

Useful Addresses

American Association of Blacks in Energy
927 15th Street NW, Suite 200
Washington, DC 20005

Museum of African American History
301 Frederick Douglass
Detroit, MI 48202

National Society of Black Physicists
c/o North Carolina A&T State University
1601 East Market Street
101 Martena Hall
Greensboro, NC 27411

**Society for Canadian Women in Science and
    Technology**
515 West Hastings Street, Room 140
Vancouver, BC V6B 5K3
Canada

Index